A Piece of String

is a wonderful thing

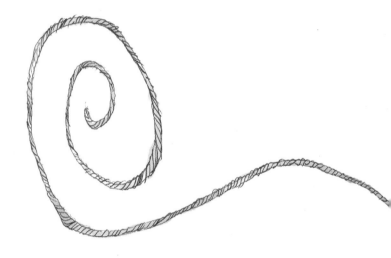

For John and Anna with love
J.H.

For Anne Veronica with love
M.C.

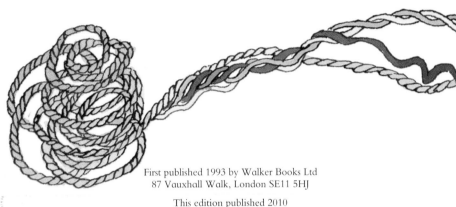

First published 1993 by Walker Books Ltd
87 Vauxhall Walk, London SE11 5HJ

This edition published 2010

2 4 6 8 10 9 7 5 3 1

Text © 1993 Judy Hindley
Illustrations © 1993 Margaret Chamberlain

The moral rights of the author and illustrator
have been asserted

This book has been typeset in Bembo Educational

Printed in China

British Library Cataloguing in Publication Data:
a catalogue record for this book is available from the British Library

ISBN 978-1-4063-1863-0

www.walker.co.uk

2

A Piece of String

is a wonderful thing

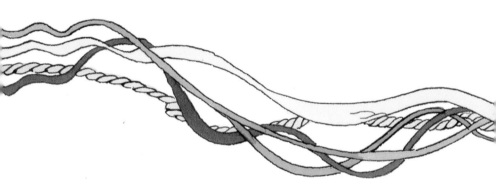

Judy Hindley

illustrated by

Margaret Chamberlain

WALKER BOOKS
AND SUBSIDIARIES
LONDON · BOSTON · SYDNEY · AUCKLAND

Let us sing a song
about string –
what a wonderful thing it is!

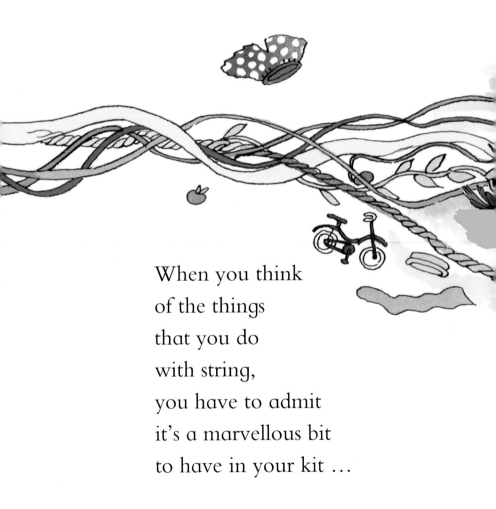

When you think
of the things
that you do
with string,
you have to admit
it's a marvellous bit
to have in your kit …

for a fishing line, a boat, a kite,
somewhere to hang your socks to dry;
for tying up parcels, fastening gates,
leading you safe through a treacherous cave;
for a spinning-top, a skipping-rope,
a bracelet, a necklace, a draw-string purse …

there's just about no end of things
a person can do with a piece of string!
And then you wonder,
from time to time,
how did a thing like
string begin?

Back in the days
when mammoths roamed,
and they didn't have chains
and they didn't have ropes
for hauling things round
or lifting them up –
(well, they didn't have any connecting things:

8

buttons or braces or buckles or laces
or latches or catches or bolts or belts,
or tabs or clasps or hooks-and-eyes …
Velcro patches! ribbons! ties!
zips or grips or snaps or clips)
well how did anyone
THINK IT UP?

Did they chat as they sat
round the fire at night,
eating their prehistoric fish,
and say, "What we need
to do it right
is a thing like hair,
but long and strong,
a thing to tie on a bit of bone:
what a wonderful fishing line
that would make!"?

After which, I suppose,
they went out to the lake
and tickled the fish
with their cold, bare hands –
for they didn't have nets
if they didn't have string.

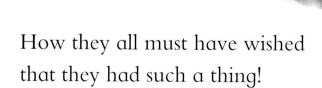

How they all must have wished
that they had such a thing!

So how on earth
do you think they discovered it?
Was it an accident? Was it a guess?
Did it emerge from a hideous mess?
Did it begin with
a sinuous twig,
a whippety willow,
a snaky vine…?

Did it happen that somebody, one dark night,
wending his weary way home alone,
got tripped by the foot on a loop of a vine
and fell, kersplat!, and bust a bone;
and then, as he lay in the dark, so sad,
and yelled for help (and it didn't come)
he got thoroughly bored with doing that
and invented – a woolly-rhinoceros trap?

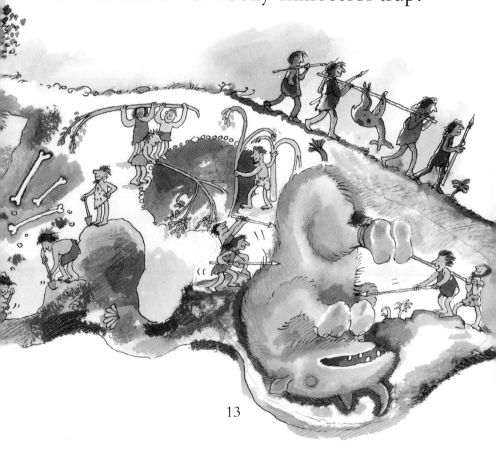

Oh, it might have occurred
in a number of ways
as the populace pondered
the fate they faced –
as they huddled in caves
in the worst of the weather,
wishing for things like tents
and clothes,
as they hugged bits of fur
to their shivery bodies
and scraps of skins
to their cold,
bare toes.

And they didn't have braces
or poppers or laces
or buttons or toggles
or grips or pins –
so HOW did they hold up their trousers, then?
They must have said,
"Oh! a piece of string
would be SUCH a fine thing
to have around the cave!"

They needed a noose for an antelope foot.
They needed a thing to string a bow.
They needed nets, and traps, and snares
for snaffling rabbits unawares
and leading the first wild horses home…
Well, they must've gone on to try and try
as thousands and thousands of years went by …

twisting and plaiting
and trying out knots
with strips of hide
and rhinoceros guts,
spiders' webs
and liana vines,

reeds and weeds and ribs of palm,
slippery sinews, thews and thongs,
elephant grasses three feet long
and wriggly fish–bone skeletons…

17

And they spun out the fibres
of vegetable fluff
and they felted the hairs of a goat,
and they knitted and twisted
and plaited and twined …

and invented …

the three-ply rope!
What a wonderful thing!
A very fine thing!
The KING of string
is rope!

Making rope

One man twists two strands clockwise and walks forward.

A second man makes sure the strands of rope are laid tightly together.

A third man closes the strands by twisting this tool anticlockwise and walks backwards as the rope is formed.

You can lift up pots
from an echoing well with it,
fling it to make a bridge;
you can haul along
hulking hunks of stone
for building a pyramid

… and they did.

You can also halter and harness
your animal friends…

And then again, when life gets tough
and it's time to be moving along,
you can use it to lash your luggage fast
to a camel, a goat, a raft, a boat –

oh! a stringable thing
is the only thing
to have when you're afloat!

But they still
went on and on,
sticking and spinning
and looping and gluing

early cart

pontoon bridge

24

Roman crane

and tying and trying out
more and more types,
faster and faster
and possibly madder

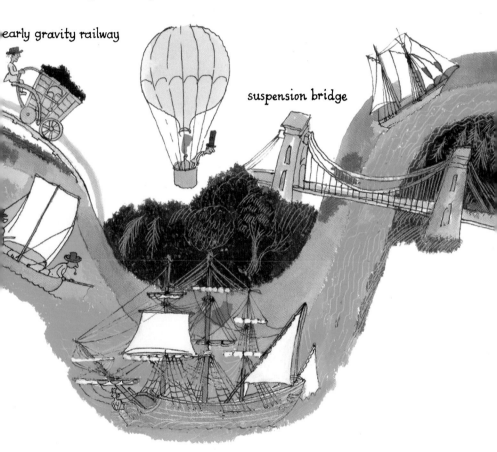

early gravity railway

suspension bridge

for pulleys and ladders and hoses and bridges
and fences and winches and wires and pipes.

Where on earth
have we got to now?
What would a town
ever do without string
and things that go stringing along?
Candlewicks, rackets and violins,
telephones, plumbing and railways lines,
things that fasten and fuse and fix
and click and stick and link…

Can you even begin to count the ways
that things connect with other things?
It could just about scramble your brain!

And to think it began
(though we'll never know when)
with somebody choking
on elephant gristle,
or trying to chew
through the stem of a thistle,
or just stumbling into
the thing!

Oh, what we've done with a piece of string
is a marvellous thing, an amazing thing –
some would say a crazy thing!
And maybe one day
we should dream up a way
to go back and start over again…

String ... and hunting

For a long time the only spears were pointed sticks.

By 2.5 million years ago, people were chipping stones to make a cutting edge.

Much later, a chip of stone would be tied to the stick with a sinew.

Sinews are "living strings" – like elastic – that help humans
and animals
to move.

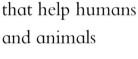

In time, ancient hunters learned to use sinews to string their bows.

antler
harpoon

antler
spearhead

Another hunting breakthrough was the bolas – three stones tied to a leather strap or a sinew. It was whirled round an animal's legs to trip it up.

String ... and clothes

The first clothes were animal skins and
the very first needles were probably thorns.

Later on, the first fabric was made by
weaving and knitting yarn. Yarn can be
spun from sheep's fleece, cotton tufts or
even birds' down.

A single fibre of wool (sheep's fleece) is
as strong as a thread
of gold.

String ... and the Egyptians

The oldest rope ever discovered came from a tomb in Egypt. It was made from flax 5,000 years ago. The Egyptians also made rope from bulrushes and camel hair. Sometimes rope was even made from women's hair.

Rope can be used for:

measuring a field

carrying water

making sure stone is flat –

or straight with a plumb-line

More about string

In New Guinea, people make fishing nets out of spiders' webs. They leave a wooden frame with a colony of spiders, who spin their webs around it. Once in a museum, I even saw a spiders' web hat that was made this way.

Tying knots in rope and string lets us do many wonderful things.

A slip knot can hitch a boat, a horse, a swing.

String can be used to send messages.

three small knots   three big knots   three small knots

= ··· − − − ··· = Morse code for S.O.S.

Hot metal can be stretched into rails and cables, ropes and delicate wires, which were used in early flying machines.

The famous Clifton Suspension Bridge in Bristol is made of metal ropes. The inventor, Isambard Kingdom Brunel, had to use a hot-air balloon to lay the first rope.

String can be made of...

willow

palm

strips of hide

liana vines

a fish bone
skeleton

grasses

twigs

bulrushes

37

Index

There are 10 titles in the
READ AND DISCOVER series.
Which ones have you read?

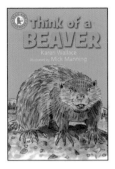

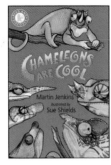

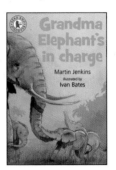

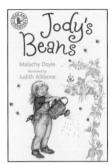

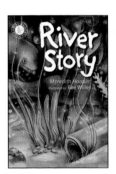

Available from all good booksellers

www.walker.co.uk

FOR THE BEST CHILDREN'S BOOKS, LOOK FOR THE BEAR.